Where are We Going?

In 1986 our ministry developed a unique biblical worldview assessment tool called the PEERS Test. The assessment was designed to reflect an individual's basic 'worldview position' in five key areas of life: Politics, Economics, Education, Religion and Social Issues (P-E-E-R-S). Using a scale of +100 to -100, results of the 70-item test ranked the individual into one of four worldview categories- Biblical Theism (70-100), Moderate Christian (30-69), Secular Humanism (0-29) and Socialism (scores less than 0). The PEERS test has been through several forms of validity measurements most significantly a professionally conducted Validity & Reliability study performed in 1995. In all cases the PEERS Test has received high marks as a valid instrument for the measurement of 'worldview' understanding.

In 1988, the Institute began tracking PEERS results of high school youth from three distinct education settings: 1) Public schools, 2) Traditional Christian schools and 3) Worldview-based Christian schools. Worldview-based Christian schools were distinguished from Traditional Christian schools in that in addition to common aspects of Christian education such as a Bible class and weekly chapel services, these schools have either a worldview class in the same manner as an English class or Algebra class (or an emphasis on worldview understanding in all major subjects) plus special in-service training for faculty members on the subject of worldview and to varying degrees, worldview training provided to the parent body.

While it is not an exact science to classify Christian schools as either Traditional or Worldview-based, the Institute has

1

never been able to classify more than 10% of its school population as the latter. As of this writing (2011) approximately 900 schools have used testing materials from Nehemiah Institute in one form or another. The high majority of schools being classified as 'worldview' are schools with membership in one of two particular Christian schools associations: Association of Classical & Christian Schools (ACCS) or Foundation for American Christian Education (FACE). Usually these schools will have a dual membership by being members of another Christian school association such as Association of Christian Schools, Int. (ACSI) or Christian Schools, Int. (CSI).

PEERS results of youth from public schools was obtained primarily (at least 90%) by testing youth groups in evangelical churches where a high percentage of the youth group were attending public schools. Occasionally PEERS testing would be conducted of a full public school class when a doctoral student received permission to give the PEERS test to an entire class of students to obtain research data for his/her dissertation paper. The Institute has aided approximately 20 graduate students in this manner.

PEERS results from these three particular high school settings have been tracked since 1988. With 20 years of assessment data, from approximately 60,000 students, the following results have occurred:

	1988	2011	change/ year	
Public school students	38.9	6.0	-1.43	points
Traditional Christian schools	49.7	15.1	-1.50	"
Worldview-based schools	62.1	70.4	+0.36	"

In all three groups the results have varied year-to-year with slight increases or decreases, but with noticeably consistent trend lines.

Homeschool students generally have ranged between the Traditional Christian school students and the Worldview-based school students, average score for high school level at 48.65 for the past three years. A small percentage of home school students have scored very well, above 80.0 (about 8%) but a surprisingly higher percentage score low, less than 30.0 (about 25%).

Using this classification of schools and the assessment data of each group, it is the position of Nehemiah Institute that at least 90% of youth from Christian homes are attending either public schools or traditional Christian schools and are consistently abandoning the Christian worldview in favor of the Humanist/ Socialist worldview. Results are fairly good in the worldview-based schools but the rate of improvement could be stronger. It is estimated that there are less than 500 'worldview-based' Christian schools in the U.S. out of the approximately 12,000 private Christian & parochial schools in existence. These trends do not bode well for the health of the Christian church in America over the next 20-40 years.

In 2001 the Nehemiah Institute published a report stating the following:

> If the PEERS trends of high school youth from Christian homes continues at the same rate of decline (those in Traditional Christian schools or in public schools), we would have to officially label the 'next generation of Christian adults' as "Committed Secular Humanists with leanings toward Socialism" between the years 2014 and 2018.

Please note, this was not a forecast or a 'prophecy' but simply stating that **if the same rate of decline** continued then the PEERS scores of these two groups would fall below -10.0 on average by 2014 for youth in public schools and by 2018 in Traditional Christian schools, which would give strong support for their views being firmly grounded in basic tenets of Humanism and/or Socialism.

Now, seven years later, with the exact same test, and the addition of several thousand test results, the following calculation can be made:

> Assuming the **same rate of decline** in test scores of the past seven years, students from 'traditional Christian schools' would score on average at -9.9 in the year 2016. Youth from Christian homes and attending public schools would score -24.5 in the same year.

These results, remarkably close to the view seen in 2001, would mean that the students had intentionally rejected the basic tenets of Biblical Theism in favor of basic tenets of Humanism/Socialism. In short, it means that the secularization of our culture has more successfully captured the hearts and minds of *our youth* than has the efforts of the Christian home, the church or even the traditional Christian school. With 90% of youth from Christian homes being among this group, it seems clear that the Christian Church could be in for a major collapse in the first half of the 21st century, based on historical orthodox views of Christianity.

As a side note, I have stated for years that the decade of 1910-1919 would likely be identified as perhaps the most troublesome decade in our history due to several unbiblical polices put in place, not the least being the creation of the Federal Reserve System, passing the 16th Amendment (direct income tax), and passing the 17th

Amendment, change of electing U.S. Senators by popular vote rather than by state-appointment, as had been the case since the ratification of the constitution. All of these were adopted in 1913.

It would not surprise me to see the decade of 2010-2019 (one hundred years later) be the decade of our undoing. Hopefully, and prayerfully, we will get it right during the second half of the 21st century.

When writing this article, a rather remarkable thing happened. I recalled a book that I read several years ago which proved instrumental in my thoughts about developing a 'worldview test.' The book is, <u>Suicide of the West</u>, by Dr. James Burnham, 1985. I have referenced this book off and on, as I generally do with several books in my library. Because of the subject matter of this article, I felt compelled to re-read Dr. Burnham's book and was more than a little surprised at some of his statements. *Suicide of the West* is one of a handful of books which I regularly challenge Christian schools to make as mandatory reading by their faculty.

The primary thesis of Dr. Burnham's important book is that cultures can and do 'commit suicide' by buying into particular ideologies (which Dr. Burnham identifies as *Liberalism*) that simply do not work long term. He stated, *"This book is a set of variations on a single and simple underlying thesis": that what Americans call "liberalism" is the ideology of Western suicide."* P. 26

It was Dr. Burnham's opinion, in the 1980's, that Western Civilization was far down the road toward this tragic ending. Here are some of the comments that caught my eye in light of what I am presenting in this paper:

"The contradiction of the West cannot be explained by any lack of economic resources or of military and political power. We must conclude that the primary causes of the contraction of the West-not the sole causes, but the sufficient and determining causes- have been internal and non-quantitative: involving either structural changes or intellectual, moral and spiritual factors." P.23, 24

"Even today, [1985] *when the Western dominion has been cut to less than half of what it was in 1914, Western economic resources- real and available resources- and Western military power are still far superior to those of the non-Western regions."* P. 23 Comment: I find it interesting that Dr. Burnham chose this year, 1914, the middle of the decade I referred to above, as a time from which the Western world has shrunk in influence.

"If the process continues over the next several decades more or less as it has gone on during the several decades just past, then [his emphasis] *– this is a merely mathematical extrapolation- the West will be finished; Western civilization, Western societies and nations in any significant and recognizable sense, will just not be there anymore. In that event, it will make a reasonable amount of sense to say: 'The West committed suicide'."* P. 24, 25 Comment: Dr. Burnham's reference to 'the next several decades,' written in the early 1980's, could fit nicely with the decade of 2010-2019 I referred to as the 'decade of our undoing.'

Another important voice at about the same time was Francis Schaeffer. In 1981 Dr. Schaeffer stated in his Christian Manifesto, *"At this moment we are in a humanistic culture, but we are happily not in a totally humanistic culture. But what we must realize is that the drift has been all in this direction. If it is not turned around*

6

we will move very rapidly into a <u>totally</u> [his emphasis]
humanistic culture."   P. 49 *"The failed responsibility*
covers a wide swath. Christian educators, Christian
theologians, Christian lawyers- none of them blew loud
trumpets until we were a long, long way down the road
toward a humanistically based culture." P. 50

One can only surmise what Dr. Schaeffer would say today
about our culture. But it seems safe to say that given what
has happened in our churches (flirting with endorsing the
homosexual life style), breakdown of the public school
system, humanism in the Christian schools, widespread
immorality on TV, corruption at the highest levels of civil
government, etc., etc., it seems likely he would say
'humanism has totally captured our culture.'

All of this begs the question- Where are we going? Are we
still on the journey to be a 'city on a hill,' envisioned by the
Puritans and Pilgrims? Are we forsaking that idea in favor
of a total secular culture not wed to absolute dogma? Are
we seeking to bring about a new kind of humanity? A new
religion? Or, are we simply confused and lost, and really
don't know where we are going?

As Christians, with absolute truth and in relationship with
the God of the universe, we better take seriously His
command to "Go therefore and make disciples of all
nations." Our spiritual capital has nearly been spent- we
are almost bankrupt.

The first question we must answer, I believe, is What
should we be doing about the secularization of our youth?
If we cannot answer this question, with clarity and
conviction, then it seems certain that we as a Christian
community and as a nation, are severely confused and will
suffer the consequences of being a prodigal son.

It is clear that the Christian school movement of the past 40 years and the homeschooling movement of the past 20+ years are having only marginal impact on the next generation of the Christian community. With 85% of the Christian community still enrolling their children into the officially self-proclaiming humanist public school system, it seems clear that we have a long way to go in understanding the clear command of Scripture to 'train them up in the way they should go.'

Following is a chapter from our larger study on philosophy of education:

Overview of Prevailing Worldviews

Objectives:

- To demonstrate that all people in society have an established worldview

- To explore the fundamental concepts of society's four major worldviews

- To confirm why a biblical worldview is the only valid worldview

- To teach you the definitions of key worldview terms

- To help you develop a biblical worldview in five distinct areas of your life

Key Terms: You will find the definitions to each key term at the end of this lesson.

Worldview	Philosophy
Theology	Secularism
Materialism	Marxism
Pragmatism	Existentialism
Hedonism	Pantheism
Panentheism	Deism
Atheism	Polytheism
Theism	Nihilism
Conservatism	Liberalism

Biblical Support:

Casting down imaginations, and every high thing that exalteth itself against the knowledge of God, and bringing into captivity every thought to the obedience of Christ (II Corinthians 10:5)

Point: Everything we believe and the thoughts that enter our mind should be brought before God. This means we should have a strong working knowledge of scripture, preventing us from being deceived by the lies of Satan. The verse above shows there is no such thing as "neutral ground" or "gray areas." Through scripture, Christ gives clear teaching that He has an "opinion" as to what is correct and incorrect regarding our thoughts.

But now, after that ye have known God, or rather are known of God, how turn ye again to the weak and beggarly elements, whereunto ye desire again to be in bondage? (Galatians 4:9)

9

Point: In coming to Christ, knowing God, and being known by God, we are to experience a living transformation realizing how our past life was weak and worthless. Through hearing God's Word, coupled with prayer, fellowship, and Bible study, we should experience increasing freedom to become all that God has intended us to be. We must know God's ways so we do not yield to the desires of the flesh that would only enslave us to the works and lies of Satan.

The wicked, through the pride of his countenance, will not seek after God: God is not in all his thoughts. (Psalm 10:4)

But the natural man receiveth not the things of the Spirit of God: for they are foolishness unto him: neither can he know them, because they are spiritually discerned. (I Corinthians 2:14)

Point: The verses above speak to the vast difference between a **natural man** (unsaved) and a **spiritual man** (saved). Scripture says the natural man cannot receive spiritual things. Unless God first works a change in the heart of the natural man, he will remain enslaved to thinking naturally throughout his life. When a person's heart becomes enlightened (also known as quickened, new birth, or born-again) by the Holy Spirit, he can now receive and understand spiritual truth from scripture. The natural man and the spiritual man live in two different worlds with differing worldviews.

Cardinal John Henry Newman (1801–1890)

"O wisdom of the world! And strength of the world! What are you when matched beside the foolishness and the weakness of the Christian? You are great in resources, manifold in methods, hopeful in prospects; but one thing you have not -- and that is peace. You are always tumultuous, restless, apprehensive. You have nothing you can rely upon. You have no rock under your feet. The humblest, feeblest Christian has that which is impossible to you."

Point: Prior to our conversion to Christ, we were only capable of having a secular humanist worldview. Though fallen man knows that God exists (Romans 1:18-20), man lives his life as if *"there is no God to whom I am accountable."* Fallen men do not seek God and do not desire God, leading to a strong **man-centered** worldview which believers in Christ must overcome by prayer and study of scripture.

For my thoughts are not your thoughts, neither are your ways my ways, saith the LORD. For as the heavens are higher than the earth, so are my ways higher than your ways, and my thoughts than your thoughts. (Isaiah 55:8, 9)

Point: In his fallen state, man and God live in mutually exclusive realms. We do not think God's thoughts, and we do not behave as He would. God is completely righteous; we are completely unrighteous (in all areas of life). Coming to Christ means we must learn to think and behave in new ways. In other words, as a new creature in Christ we will need a new belief set; a **new worldview**.

Sow to yourselves in righteousness, reap in mercy; break up your fallow ground: for it is time to seek the LORD, till he come and rain righteousness upon you. Ye have plowed wickedness, ye have reaped iniquity; ye have eaten the fruit of lies: because thou didst trust in thy way, in the multitude of thy mighty men. (Hosea 10:12, 13)

Point: Before Christ we lived life on our own terms. We planned, dreamed and acted as if we held fate in our hands, and determined our own life experiences. We were the captain of our ship and proud of it. But God says that we only produced wickedness, ate the fruit of lies, and consequently reaped the due punishment for the error of our ways.

Now, in Christ, we are to sow, reap and seek with an understanding that Christ alone is righteous. Our lives should be lived with the intent of bringing glory to Him. How can we do this unless we know His ways? We must have a clear biblical view of life.

Worldview -- a growing "buzzword" in education

"Worldview" is a topic of increasing importance to Christians. As our nation witnesses an increasing assault against truth, the demise of moral values, the breakdown of the family and social order, many are asking, *"What has happened to our nation?"* As Christians, we must take action to counter the secularization of our culture. For the sake of the Lord's name, and for the well-being of our posterity, we can no longer allow anti-Christian philosophy to rule our land.

For there are many unruly and vain talkers and deceivers, specially they of the circumcision whose <u>mouths must be stopped</u>, who subvert whole houses, teaching things which they ought not, for filthy lucre's sake. (Titus 1:10, 11)

Lesson:

I. What is a "Worldview?"

1. What is God?
2. What is man?
3. What is God's desire for man?
4. What is the chief end of man?

A. Worldview definitions by respected authors and leaders

1. <u>Understanding the Times</u>, Dr. David Noebel

    a. "The term *worldview* refers to any ideology, philosophy, theology, movement, or religion that provides an overarching approach to understanding God, the world, and man's relations to God and the world. Specifically, a worldview should contain a particular perspective regarding each of the following ten disciplines: theology, philosophy, ethics, biology, psychology, sociology, law, politics, economics, and history." [1]

2. Worldviews in Conflict, Dr. Ronald Nash

   a. "In simplest terms, a worldview is a set of beliefs about the most important issues in life." [2]

   b. "It is sadly ironic that the basic features of the naturalistic worldview, which so many people in the formerly Marxist nations are now rejecting, remain attractive to great numbers of educated people in the West."

   c. "One major reason for this, I am convinced, is that few Americans have been taught to think in terms of worldviews. They do not know what a worldview is; they could not spell out

---

Session II
[1] David A. Noebel, *Understanding the Times*, (Eugene, OR: Harvest House Publishers, 1994), p. 8.
[2] Ronald H. Nash, *Worldviews in Conflict*, (Grand Rapids, MI: Zondervan Publishing House, 1992), p. 16.

the content of their own worldview if their lives depended on it; they are unaware of how various aspects of conflicting worldviews clash logically." [3]

d. "During the first several decades of this century, conflicts in the world of ideas seemed removed from the everyday life of the average Christian. Those battles were usually fought in academic circles -- the more prominent colleges and universities, and in theological seminaries. Back then, when smaller numbers of Americans attended college, many average Christians tended to give little thought to these issues.

e. That inattention carried a high price tag, however. Eventually, the anti-Christian ideas that gained dominance in America's intellectual centers filtered down to many theological seminaries and finally took hold in the religion departments of many church-related colleges. It is sad that the process continues today, as many informed observers of self-described evangelical colleges and seminaries report.

f. That unbelief also reached the pulpits of a number of formerly faithful churches. Because many people in the pews were theologically illiterate or indifferent, the fact that some pastors were now preaching a new gospel -- one that denied practically every major tenet of New Testament faith went unnoticed.

---

[3] Ibid, p. 9

g.   America's mainline denominations were lost
to and unbelief because liberalism in the
century following the American Civil War the
Christian church lost the battle in the world
of ideas.

Dorothy L. Sayers (1893–1957)

*"God... has created us perfectly free to disbelieve
in him as much as we choose. If we do disbelieve,
then He and we must take the consequences in a
world ruled by cause and effect."*

h. The most important step for Christians is to
become informed about the Christian
worldview, a comprehensive systematic view
of the life and of the world as a whole.

i. No believer today can be really effective in the
arena of ideas until he or she has been
trained to think in worldview terms. How
does the Christian worldview differ from
worldviews of the enemy? What are the
weaknesses of competing worldviews? How
can we utilize the best arguments against
them?" [4]

j. Major elements of a worldview:

"A well-rounded worldview includes beliefs
in at least five major areas: **God**, **reality**,
knowledge, **morality**, and **humankind**." [5]

---

[4] Ibid., p 13,14.
[5] Ibid., p. 26.

1) <u>God</u> -- the most important element of any worldview is
what that worldview says or does not say about God.

2) <u>Reality</u> -- is the existence of the universe an undeniable fact? Is the universe eternal? Did an eternal, personal, omnipotent God create the world? Is there a purpose in the universe? Are miracles possible?

3) <u>Knowledge</u> -- is truth relative or must truth be the same for all rational beings? What is the relationship between religious faith and reason? Is knowledge about God possible?

4) <u>Ethics</u> -- are there moral laws that govern human conduct? Are these moral laws the same for all mankind? Does it make sense to say that some action may be right for people in one culture and wrong for others?

5) <u>Humankind</u> -- are human beings free? What is the human soul or mind, and how does it relate to the body? Does physical death end the existence of the human person? Are there rewards and punishments after death?

These questions must be biblically answered by the Christian in order to be a credible witness for Christ.

3. <u>Coalition on Revival Documents</u>, Dr. Jay Grimstead

    a. We affirm that the Bible is God's statements to us regarding religion, salvation, eternity, and righteousness. Scripture is the final measurement and collection of certain fundamental facts of reality and basic principles that God wants all mankind to know in the spheres of law, government, economics, business, education, arts and communication, medicine, psychology, and science.

    b. All theories and practices of these spheres of life are only true, right, and realistic when they agree with the Bible.

 Abraham Lincoln, 1809 – 1865 (16th U.S. President) *"I believe the Bible is the best gift God has ever given to men. All the good from the Savior of the world is communicated to us through this Book."*

    c. "The Bible furnishes mankind with the only logical and verbal connection between time and eternity, religion and science, the visible and invisible worlds." [6]

[6] Jay Grimstead, Foundations: The Christian Worldview Series, A Manifesto for the Christian Church, 1986, p. 10.

d. "We affirm that the Bible presents God's own worldview, which is consistent and practical and answers all of the basic life questions of man.

e. To function properly in the Church and in the world, Christians must seek to understand, to the best of their ability, the full theological worldview presented in the Bible.

f. They must be willing to measure all points of their own theology by the Bible and, in submission to the Bible, to make whatever changes are called for in their own theology." [7]

II. Why is Possessing and Understanding a Christian Worldview so Important?

A. God demands it

This day the LORD thy God hath commanded thee to do these statutes and judgments: thou shalt therefore keep and do them with all thine heart, and with all thy soul. (Deuteronomy 26:16)

Casting down imaginations, and every high thing that exalteth itself against the knowledge of God, and bringing into captivity every thought to the obedience of Christ; (II Corinthians 10:5)

For my thoughts are not your thoughts, neither are your ways my ways, saith the LORD. For as

---

[7] Ibid., p. 10,11.

*the heavens are higher than the earth, so are my
ways higher than your ways, and my thoughts
than your thoughts.* (Isaiah 55:8, 9)

*Sow to yourselves in righteousness, reap in mercy;
break up your fallow ground: for it is time to seek
the LORD, till he come and rain righteousness
upon you. Ye have plowed wickedness, ye have
reaped iniquity; ye have eaten the fruit of lies:
because thou didst trust in thy way, in the
multitude of thy mighty men.* (Hosea 10:12, 13)

Point: Man is created in the image of God; therefore, it
is logical man should reflect God's character and
nature in his day-to-day living. Due to the fall of
man, however, and the resulting sinful nature
carried by him, man is unable to know God and
cannot desire to be like Him. Out of graciousness,
God provided written instructions (The Law)
enabling men to know the right decision to make
in all life situations.

Apart from a new birth relationship with God
through Jesus Christ, the Law only serves to
make us aware of our sinfulness. The Law is a
constant reminder that we are wholly
incapable of pleasing God and that His wrath
rests upon us.

For those who place their trust in Jesus Christ's
death on the cross as the atonement for sin, the
Holy Spirit reveals God's Law to them, and
empowers them to live according to its
requirements. This pleases God. He bestows His
favor on believers, resulting in their
sanctification, peace, and works of righteousness.

B. **Society needs a Christian worldview**

1. Turning Point -- A Christian Worldview Declaration, Herbert Schlossberg

    a. "American Christianity is at a turning point. We face perhaps the greatest challenge, and the greatest opportunity, since the founding of our country. The challenge we face is the tidal wave of militant anti-Christian belief engulfing society and the chaos it leaves in its wake: the AIDS epidemic, the dissolution of the family, the abortion holocaust, growing economic weakness, the crisis of judge-made law, teen pregnancy, and widespread financial fraud.

    b. These difficult problems and many others are largely the by-product of the humanist idea that man is the measure of all things and that all ethical standards are relative. Frequently proposed 'solutions' (for example, 'safe sex' and school based clinics) and ideological fixes (liberal statism, atheistic libertarianism, radical feminism) are proven failures or disasters waiting to happen.

    c. It is becoming painfully apparent that anti-Christian humanism, the guiding force of our society for the last three decades, [now four] does

21

not work. The world is in crisis and people want answers. Christianity -- which is not an ideology but the truth about God, man, and the world provides the answers people want and need." [8]

2. Summit Ministries

   a. *"Nothing short of a great Civil War of Values rages today throughout North America,"* say James Dobson and Gary Bauer. "Two sides with vastly differing and incompatible worldviews are locked in a bitter conflict that permeates every level of society."

   b. To be more precise, it is a battle between worldviews. On one side is the Christian worldview. On the other is the Humanistic worldview divided into three easily definable branches: **Secular Humanism**, **Marxism/Leninism**, and **Cosmic Humanism** (or the New Age movement).

   c. *"Someday soon,"* Dobson and Bauer say, *"a winner* [in the battle for our children's hearts and minds] *will emerge and the loser will fade from memory."* For now, the outcome is very much in doubt. In order to emerge victorious, Christians

---

[8] Herbert Schlossberg, *Turning Point*, (Wheaton, IL: Crossway Books, 1987) p. 7.

must quickly arrive at an understanding of the times and take action." [9]

And of the children of Issachar, which were men that had understanding of the times, to know what Israel ought to do; the heads of them were two hundred; and all their brethren were at their commandment.
(I Chronicles 12:32)

III. Four Major Worldviews

A. Secular Humanism

1. The belief that self-proclaimed, self-ruling man begins from himself and creates his own world of truth, meaning, and value out of his own reason and experience -- without any reliance upon divine revelation.

B. Marxist/Leninist

1. A state (government) system denying the personal importance of property and thought.

2. The state has supreme authority. The state controls and owns all assets, and wields extreme limited freedom to individuals, families, churches, and businesses.

---

[9] David A. Noebel, *Understanding the Times*, (Eugene, OR: Harvest House Publishers, 1994), p. 7,8.

3. All human personality must become subject to state control.

4. All rule is enacted by power through brute force; liberty of conscience is an enemy of the state.

C. Cosmic Humanism/New Age

1. A worldview based in mysticism and monism -- "all is one." The common vision and belief of a "coming new age," with "peace and mass enlightenment."

2. A second assumption that ultimate reality is "being." It is a belief of bliss and awareness that an impersonal, infinite, consciousness rules all that exist.

3. All that is can form into individual droplets of consciousness, and because you are part of all that is, you have literally always been, yet there was an instant when that individual energy current that is you was formed. (Ocean/cup theory)

D. Biblical Christianity

1. God, a personal, infinite Supreme Being, perfect in all ways, creating the world from nothing, imputing value to creatures according to His good pleasure, demands worship,

sacrifice, and obedience to Himself alone.

2. God providentially created, rules, judges and redeems His creation totally and strictly according to His pleasure, for the sole purpose of bringing glory to Himself.

3. God chose to reveal Himself in three primary ways:

- Generally, in creation (the world)

    The heavens declare the glory of God; and the firmament showeth his handiwork. Day unto day uttereth speech, and night unto night showeth knowledge. (Psalms 19:1, 2)

    For the invisible things of him from the creation of the world are clearly seen, being understood by the things that are made, even his eternal power and Godhead; so that they are without excuse: (Romans 1:20)

- Specifically, in His Word (the Bible)

    And the LORD appeared again in Shiloh: for the LORD revealed himself to Samuel in Shiloh by the word of the LORD. (I Samuel 3:21)

    For whatsoever things were written aforetime were written for our learning, that we through patience and comfort of the scriptures might have hope. (Romans 15:4)

- Redemptively, in flesh (Jesus Christ).

    Who hath saved us, and called us with an holy calling, not according to our works, but according to his own purpose and grace, which was given us in Christ Jesus before the world began, But is now made manifest by the appearing of our Saviour Jesus Christ, who hath abolished death, and hath brought life and immortality to light through the gospel: (II Timothy 1:9,10)

IV. What are the Consequences of False Worldviews?

A. No morality

> *In those days there was no king in Israel: every man did that which was right in his own eyes.* (Judges 21:25)

B. No science

1. Greeks--
   "...looked upon the natural world largely as an exercise for the magnificent Greek reason -- the world was not to be changed, but simply to be understood." [10]

2. Muslims--
   "...everything is fatalistically determined, obviously there is no point in trying to manipulate the natural world to change anything

---

[10] D. James Kennedy, *What if Jesus Had Never Been Born?*, (Nashville, TN: Thomas Nelson Publishers, 1994), p. 93.

because all things are
unchangeable." [11]

3. Africans--
    "...animists would never have begun
    to experiment on the natural world
    since everything, whether stones or
    trees or animals or anything else
    contains within it living spirits of
    various gods or ancestors." [12]

4. Hindus--
    "...both Hinduism and Buddhism
    teach that the physical world is
    unreal and that the only reality is
    that of the world's soul and that the
    greatest thing any one has to learn
    is that the physical world is not
    real." [13]

Science could not have come out of
these worldviews because of their
irrational concepts of God and the
universe. D. James Kennedy said, "*It
[science] waited for Christianity to come
and take several of the different strains
and weave them together to produce in
the sixteenth century the phenomenon
we know as modern science. It was
because of a number of basic teachings
of Christianity.*

---

[11] Ibid., p. 94.
[12] Ibid., p. 95.
[13] Ibid., p. 95.

First of all is the fact that there is a rational God who is the source of all truth, and that this world is a rational world. This gave rise to the possibility of scientific laws." [14]

Paul Dirac (1902 – 1984)
Prior to his death in 1984, Paul Dirac was called "the world's greatest living physicist." His pioneering discoveries led to the Nobel Prize in physics in 1933 and led to the study of quantum mechanics. Called by some the equal of Isaac Newton and Albert Einstein, at age 30 he became the youngest person ever to hold a professorship at Cambridge University.

Dirac believed that God used "beautiful mathematics" to create the world. *"Beautiful, but not simple. My theories are based on faith that there is reason for all the numbers nature provides us with."* When Dirac was asked once why gravitational forces were getting weaker, he responded, *"Why? Because God made it so."* Dirac insisted that science and religion were not at odds; rather, *"they are both seekers after truth."*

---

[14] Ibid., p. 95

C. No redemption

Jesus saith unto him, I am the way, the truth, and the life: no man cometh unto the Father, but by me. (John 14:6)

Let Israel hope in the LORD: for with the LORD there is mercy, and with him is plenteous redemption. (Psalm 130:7)

Blessed be the Lord God of Israel; for he hath visited and redeemed his people,
(Luke 1:68)

D. No peace, ever

And the burden of the LORD shall ye mention no more: for every man's word shall be his burden; for ye have perverted the words of the living God, of the LORD of hosts our God. Thus shalt thou say to the prophet, What hath the LORD answered thee? and, What hath the LORD spoken?

But since ye say, The burden of the LORD; therefore thus saith the LORD; Because ye say this word, The burden of the LORD, and I have sent unto you, saying, Ye shall not say, The burden of the LORD; Therefore, behold, I, even I, will utterly forget you, and I will forsake you, and the city that I gave you and your fathers, and cast you out of my presence: And I will bring an everlasting reproach upon

*you, and a perpetual shame, which shall
not be forgotten.* (Jeremiah 23:36-40)

*Then shall he say also unto them on the
left hand, Depart from me, ye cursed,
into everlasting fire, prepared for the
devil and his angels:* (Matthew 25:41)

Jonathan Edwards (1703-1758)
*"The use of this awful subject may be for
awakening unconverted persons to a
conviction of their danger. This that you
have heard is the case of every one out of Christ.
That world of misery, that lake of burning
brimstone, is extended abroad under you. There is
the dreadful pit of the glowing flames of the
wrath of God; there is hell's wide gaping mouth
open; and you have nothing to stand upon, nor
anything to take hold of, there is nothing between
you and hell but the air; it is only the power and
mere pleasure of God that holds you up."*

The above quote from Jonathan Edwards was
taken from his famous sermon, <u>Sinners in the
hands of an angry God</u>.

V. Key-Term Definitions

Worldview:

1. The overall perspective from which one sees and interprets the world.

2. A collection of beliefs about life and the universe held by an individual or a group.

3. Any ideology, philosophy, theology, movement, or religion that provides an overarching approach to understanding God and His world, or

4. A set of presuppositions (assumptions which may be true, partially true or entirely false) which we hold (consciously or subconsciously, consistently or inconsistently) about the basic make-up of our world.

Theism:

Theism is the belief or acknowledgment of the existence of a god. Theism is diametrically opposed to atheism. Theism, however, differs from deism. Deism implies a belief in the existence of a god, yet it signifies in modern usage a denial of revelation. Theism does not deny revelation.

Philosophy:

1. Literally, the love of wisdom. In modern usage, philosophy is a general term denoting an explanation of the reasons of things; or an investigation of the causes of all phenomena of both mind and matter.

31

2. The objective of philosophy is to ascertain facts or truth, and to discover the causes of things or their phenomena; to enlarge our views of God and His works, and to render our knowledge of both practically useful and subservient to human happiness. True religion and true philosophy must ultimately arrive at the same principle.

Theology:

1. Divinity; the science of God and divine things; or the science which teaches the existence, character and attributes of God, His laws and government, the doctrines we are to believe, and the duties we are to practice. Theology consists of two branches -- natural and revealed. <u>Natural theology</u> is the knowledge we have of God from His works by the light of nature and reason. <u>Revealed theology</u> is that which is to be learned only from revelation.

2. Moral theology teaches us the divine laws relating to our manners and actions, that is, our moral duties. Theology teaches or explains the doctrines of religion, as objects of faith.

3. Scholastic theology is that which proceeds by reasoning, or which gains knowledge of divine things from certain established principles of faith.

Conservatism:

1. An attitude or philosophy that places great emphasis on tradition. Conservatism promotes conserving (saving) traditional institutions, values, and ideas. Conservatives seek progress by keeping with proven values of the past.

2. Political conservatives today believe in the concept of limited government, with government's primary purpose being the provision of defense for the citizens and protection of individual freedoms.

3. Conservatives believe that most political and economic problems are basically moral problems and must be addressed first by emphasizing the personal responsibility of those involved rather than by legislating "corrective action" on the masses. Moral standards are seen as objective rather than subjective, typically coming from Judeo-Christian tradition, and are quite static.

4. Conservatives see a valuable connection between things such as freedom and private property, free enterprise and the gifting of individuals, self-government and small, low-financed state and federal governments, and the surrendering of a limited number of individual liberties for the benefit of the masses.

Liberalism:

1. A political and economic philosophy emphasizing freedom and equality based on a dynamic understanding of things most important to each generation. Liberals believe that mankind is "inherently good" and that most problems are the result of one's environment and **not** the result of evil actions or improper desires. Liberals places strong emphasis on social responsibility, and little emphasis on personal responsibility.

2. Liberals see the need for frequent and widespread government action to provide individuals the ideal conditions allowing them to realize their human potential. This includes action in areas such as civil rights legislation, minimum wage guarantees, unemployment insurance, government secured retirement pensions, health insurance, various other anti-poverty measures, and environmentalism.

3. Liberalism (but not necessarily all who would refer to themselves as "liberal") teaches that moral standards are highly personal and come from the natural evolution of humans into "higher" beings; moral standards must necessarily change with time. Rights of the individual are generally viewed as most important, even if requiring a sacrifice of the masses.

Atheism:

Atheists absolutely disbelieve and reject the existence of God or any supreme intelligent being. Atheism is a ferocious system that leaves nothing above us to excite awe, or around us, to awaken tenderness.

In essence: "God, you just don't exist."

Deism:

The doctrine or creed of a deist is this -- a belief or system of religious opinions of individuals who acknowledge the existence of one God, but deny divine revelation. Deism is the belief in natural religion only, or those truths in doctrine and practice which man are to discover by the light of reason, independent and exclusive of any revelation from God. Hence deism implies faithlessness and a disbelief in the divine origin of the scriptures.

In essence: "Thank you God for leaving us alone."

Existentialism:

A philosophy that emphasizes the uniqueness and isolation of the individual experience in a hostile or indifferent universe; human existence is unexplainable. Existentialism stresses freedom of choice and responsibility for the consequences of one's acts.

In essence: "Capture the moment; all you have is now."

Hedonism:

>Hedonism is the veracious pursuit and devotion to seeking sensual pleasure. The ethics of this doctrine say that only what is pleasant or has pleasant consequences is intrinsically good. Hedonists believe that behavior is motivated by the desire for pleasure and the avoidance of pain.
>
>In essence: "If it feels good, do it; life is short, get all the pleasure you can."

Secularism:

>1. Pertaining to the present world, or to things not spiritual or holy; relating to things not immediately or primarily respecting the soul, but the body; worldly-minded. The secularist seeks to make provision for the support of life, the preservation of health, the temporal prosperity of men, of states, etc.
>
>2. Secular power is that which manages and governs the temporal affairs of men, the civil or political powers; and is contra-distinguished from spiritual or ecclesiastical power.
>
>In essence: "Be all you can be."

Marxism:

>Political and economic ideas developed by Karl Marx and Friedrich Engels. This system is based on the atheistic (godless) assumption that all human experience, behavior, and history are the product of purely material forces acting upon the individual. This system should be planned and controlled by the state to eventually achieve a classless society with total equality of goods.

In essence: "A chicken in every pot, guaranteed by the government!"

Materialism:

1. The doctrine of materialists is the belief that the soul of man is not a spiritual substance distinct from matter, but that it is the result, or effect, or the organization of matter in the body.

2. A materialist is one who denies the existence of spiritual substances, and maintains that the soul of man is the result of a particular organization of matter in the body.

3. The theory or doctrine that physical well-being and worldly possessions constitute the greatest good and highest value in life.

In essence: "The one who dies with the most toys wins."

Nihilism:

1. An extreme form of skepticism that denies all existence. A doctrine holding that all values are baseless and that nothing can be known or communicated.

2. Rejection of all moral and religious values; a manifest willingness to repudiate all previous theories of morality and religious belief.

3. Belief that destruction of existing political, social institutions is necessary improvement.

In essence: "I'm not here, you're not here. Our nothingness is all that's important."

Pantheism:

1. The doctrine that the universe is God, or the system of theology maintaining that the universe is the supreme God.

2. A pantheist is one that believes the universe to be God; a name given to the followers of 17th century Dutch philosopher Baruch Spinoza. The earliest Grecian pantheist of whom we read is Orpheus.

In essence: "God is in everything; I'm God, you're God, all is God."

Panentheism:

1. This view claims that God is in everything and that everything is in God; but unlike pantheism, it holds that God is more than the universe, and God continues to develop and change as the world changes.

2. Panentheism is encountered in modern process theology, which suggests that the world and God are both in process, and in a state of flux. God is not viewed as perfect, but is in the process of achieving perfection.

In essence: "Hang in there God, you can do it!"

Pragmatism:

1. Originally developed by Charles S. Pierce and William James, pragmatism is a movement based on a doctrine that says the meaning of

an idea or a proposition lies in its observable practical consequences.

2. A practical, matter-of-fact way of approaching or assessing situations or of solving problems -- situational ethics.

In essence: "If it works, do it. The end justifies the means."

Polytheism:

A belief system that teaches the plurality of gods or invisible beings superior to man, and having an agency in the government of the world.

In essence: "I have a god, do you?"

VI. Implications for the Future

Throughout history, the philosophy for how mankind should live was primarily developed and promoted by a few key individuals. Their "worldview" shaped the principles of government, economics, education, religion, and all other main spheres of life.

When these key leaders derived their views from the Word of God, the people were blessed and societies progressed, particularly in the $1^{st} - 4^{th}$ centuries and again in the $16^{th} - 18^{th}$ centuries. When the views came from philosophers and leaders trusting in their own wisdom, the people suffered severe hardships, even the annihilation of complete civilizations. Hardships were particularly evident in the $12^{th} - 15^{th}$ centuries, and again in modern times. Many consider the

20th century to be the bloodiest century in the history of mankind.

The future of our nation hangs in the balance. The Christian worldview that shaped the birth of our nation and guided her for many decades is now being replaced with radical anti-Christian worldviews. Unless a new generation rises up and reclaims the Christian heritage of our land, the next several generations (your children and grandchildren) are likely to suffer severe consequences from the "sins of their fathers" on a national level.

We implore you to <u>take very seriously</u> the content of this course and to seek God in how He may use you to re-focus our people on the biblical view of life.

Perhaps we need a 'state of the nation' summit regarding education of youth from Christian homes. There are many warning signs that the window of opportunity to effect change may be closing on us. If you are interested in helping to pull together such a summit, attend, or just kept informed of the work, please let me know at dan@nehemiahinstitute.com. I may be contacted at 800-948-3101 if you care to discuss this.

Blessings,

Dan Smithwick

"Come, let us build that we may no longer be a reproach.—" Nehemiah 2:17b

Made in the USA
Charleston, SC
23 April 2012